Contents

Some words are shown in bold, **like this**.
You can find them in the glossary on page 23.

Who has been snapped stealing pet food?

A round, prickly body. Short legs.
A pointed snout. It's a hedgehog!

You don't need to visit the countryside
to see wild animals.